THE DEPARTMENT
OF TRANSPORT

# Channel Tunnel Rail Link
# Independent Review

## March 1993

## Samuel Montagu & Co. Limited
## and
## WS Atkins Planning Consultants

LONDON:HMSO

Samuel Montagu is a Member of the Securities and Futures Authority

# CHANNEL TUNNEL RAIL LINK: INDEPENDENT REVIEW

| Contents | Paragraph | Page |
|---|---|---|

March 1993

# CHANNEL TUNNEL RAIL LINK: INDEPENDENT REVIEW

## INTRODUCTION

### Background

1.    In October 1991, the Government announced a preferred route corridor for the Channel Tunnel Rail Link ('CTRL'), based on the easterly route; (terms which are underlined are defined in the glossary at Annex A). Union Railways Ltd ('Union Railways' or 'UR'), a wholly-owned subsidiary of BR, were asked to define a detailed alignment, along this broad corridor, to the point at which public consultation could be undertaken and the land safeguarded. Union Railways were asked to submit a report to Government by the end of 1992 with a reference case for the line of the route, plus a series of options.   In view of the scale and complexity of the project, the Secretary of State for Transport decided, in consultation with BR, that there should be an independent review ('the Review') of Union Railways' work. The purpose of this report is to describe the findings of the Review.

2.    In January 1993, BR submitted to Government *The Union Railways Report* together with a number of working papers ('the UR report'). The UR report states that it has been designed to serve two purposes: (i) to provide information to enable Government to choose the route to be taken forward for public consultation; and (ii) to provide a preliminary indication of the likely viability of the project. In submitting the report, BR indicated that further work was in hand to examine the alignment of the route of CTRL between Stratford and the London terminal.

3.    The work carried out by Union Railways on the preparation of the reference case and options has also involved staff from other parts of BR, such as staff of European Passenger Services Limited ('EPS'), Network SouthEast ('NSE') and the Kings Cross project team. For the purposes of this report, the terms 'Union Railways', 'UR', or 'the UR team' are defined to include, where the context admits, other BR staff engaged in activities which have links with the CTRL project, such as staff of EPS or NSE. The terms are also defined to include consultancy firms appointed by Union Railways to assist in developing engineering, planning and environmental aspects of the work. Figures for costs given in this report are expressed in Fourth Quarter 1992 ('4Q92') price levels.

### Terms of reference

4.    The purpose of the Review, as set out in the terms of reference issued to us (Samuel Montagu and WS Atkins) by the Department of Transport ('the Department') in June 1992, is to provide the Department with an independent assessment of whether the work carried out by Union Railways, on the preparation of the reference case and options for CTRL, has been carried out *in a reasonable way*. We have taken this to mean 'in a way which is sufficient for the purpose of taking a decision about the route to be taken forward for public consultation, and which provides financial information which is at an appropriate level of reliability, taking account of the current stage of development of the project'. The terms of reference for the Review do not include assessing the likely viability of the project in the private sector, recommending a route, or advising what action should be taken after Union Railways submit their report. A copy of our terms of reference is given in Annex B.

5.    This report is divided into six main parts:

(i)    The first part provides a summary of the conclusions.

(ii)    The second part covers the choice of the reference case and options.

(iii)    The third part covers capital costs, railway engineering requirements, operations and safety.

(iv)    The fourth part covers environmental impact.

(v)    The fifth part covers traffic and revenue forecasts, and railway operating costs.

(vi)    The sixth part covers investment appraisal.

The terms of reference for each aspect are given at the front of each part of this report.

**Approach**

6.    The approach we have taken to the Review has been broadly as follows. First, we have reviewed the approach being taken by Union Railways to each aspect of the work. Second, we have sought to identify, taking account of the experience of other major capital projects such as the Channel Tunnel (to the extent that they are relevant in this case), matters which we would need to assess in preparing this report, and to inform the Union Railways team in time for them to take them into account in their work programme. Third, we have monitored the work as it has progressed, and attended key meetings on the development of the route options. Finally, we have reviewed the UR report including relevant working papers (or explanations provided by the UR team), in the light of the matters identified earlier.

7.    Our report has been prepared as follows. Samuel Montagu has been responsible for preparing the Parts dealing with capital costs, traffic and revenue forecasts, the choice of the reference case and the investment appraisal, drawing on comments prepared by WS Atkins where appropriate. WS Atkins has been responsible for preparing the Part dealing with environmental impact, the Sections dealing with railway engineering requirements, operations and safety, and railway operating costs, and the Annexes dealing with railway engineering requirements, operations and safety, the basis of preparation of the capital cost estimates, and the reliability of the capital cost estimates and risk analysis.

8.    Our terms of reference require that the Review should address the issues at a strategic level and should not duplicate the work of the UR team. Accordingly, we have taken our investigations and our review of information to a level which we consider appropriate, and have sought such explanations from Union Railways as we consider necessary. Our views are therefore given at a strategic level, eg our view on compliance with the brief from Government relates to compliance at a strategic level.

9.    We are grateful for the cooperation we have received from the UR team in meeting us, providing information, making presentations, and responding to enquiries and requests for further information.

## SUMMARY OF CONCLUSIONS

### The process as a whole

10.   The work carried out by Union Railways on the preparation of the reference case and options for CTRL has been carried out in a way which is sufficient, in our view, for the purpose of taking a decision about the route between Stratford and Cheriton to be taken forward for public consultation.  We have commented, where appropriate, on the level of reliability of the financial information.

### Choice of reference case and options

11.   In our view, the work by Union Railways on optioneering the route (to choose the reference case and options) complies with the remit from Government; the approach taken is what we would expect; the work has been carried out in a professional manner; and the reference case and options have been developed to a level of detail which is appropriate for this stage of the project.  We consider that the work provides a suitable base for taking a decision about the route of CTRL between Stratford and Cheriton.  As noted above, further work is in hand to examine the alignment of the route of CTRL between Stratford and the London terminal.

### Capital costs

12.   Our conclusions on capital costs are shown below:

(i)   The findings on *railway engineering, operations and safety* are as follows.  The railway engineering standards (gauge, horizontal curvature, and gradient standards) adopted by UR for CTRL provide, in our view, a satisfactory basis for alignment design.  We consider that UR's approach to tunnel design is reasonable.  The design provides for potential use by freight trains, as required by the brief from Government.  The approach to railway operations is reasonable, in our view.  Safety risk assessment is being carried out in a structured fashion.

(ii)   The estimates of *capital costs for the route and on-route stations* have been prepared by Union Railways on the basis of assumptions about: (a) contract strategy; (b) the price base; (c) the design adopted for the route and stations; and (d) the project timescale and construction programme.   UR's assumptions about *contract strategy* are conventional assumptions for Government investment in major civil engineering projects.  This approach is reasonable, in our view.  UR's assumption about the *price base* is that the rates and prices derived in 1989 should be used as the basis for the current estimates.  This assumption is based on recent research, but the current level of construction activity may be too low to provide reliable statistics on rates and prices.  This should not affect the choice between routes, but could affect the reliability of the overall estimates.  The risk assessment includes a nominal allowance for this risk.  The procedures and techniques adopted by Union Railways to derive estimates of the capital costs, based on the *design adopted for the route and on-route stations* are sound, in our view, and the work appears generally to have been carried out in accordance with them. It appears to us, from an examination of selected elements of the capital cost estimates, that the work has been executed in a professional manner and is at a level commensurate with the current stage of development of the design. The UR team has assumed an outline *construction programme* which allows completion of CTRL early in the year 2000. The programme assumes that it will be possible to commit a certain level of funds and procure various work and supplies before Royal Assent (or approval under an alternative procedure) is obtained. There is a risk that it may not be possible to do so in this way; this could affect the level of reliability of the overall estimates but should not affect the choice between routes.

(iii) The UR report does not cover the Kings Cross project or describe the basis of preparation of the capital cost estimates which are given for the total cost of railway works at Kings Cross or the part of the low level station which forms the *London terminal* of CTRL. We are not therefore in a position to comment on these costs, or any risks attached to them, in this report.

(iv) The findings on *reliability of the estimates and risk analysis* are as follows. The basic estimates of the capital costs are, in our view, as reliable as they can be expected to be at this stage of the development of the design. No contingencies have been included in the estimates, but a formal risk assessment has been undertaken by UR, designed to predict the range of capital costs against a probability of achievement. A margin of error in the range of -10% to +30% is normal for a project of this type at this stage of development. The risk assessment approach adopted by UR indicates a range of -10% to +22% around the basic estimated capital cost of the Board Reference Case, within 95% confidence limits. On the basis of our high level review of the main risk areas on the capital costs of the project, we do not consider that the margin of error of the estimated capital cost should be assumed to be less than the range of -10% to +30% which is normal for a project of this type at this stage of development. This margin will need to be reviewed when detailed information on the London terminal and the construction programme is available. UR's work so far does not include a risk appraisal of the construction programme; we understand that the UR team intends shortly to carry out an assessment of the risk of delay in the programme.

**Environmental impact**

13. The approach taken by UR to appraisal of environmental impact and the development of the route to minimise adverse environmental effects at reasonable cost is, in our view, acceptable. The difficulties of defining environmental standards have been professionally addressed. We consider that Union Railways have developed a method which ensures that reasonable standards are adopted, and that they are consistent and commensurate with those used for major transport infrastructure projects. A rigorous recording and validation system has been undertaken which facilitates audit of the decision-making process at any point. Because of the nature of environmental issues, there will always be a possibility that choices made in the selection of options will be revised as a result of public consultation once the route is published, but this is a normal feature of the planning process.

**Traffic and revenue forecasts**

14.    Our conclusions on the approach to traffic and revenue forecasts and their reliability are as follows:

(i)    The approach to forecasting *international passenger* traffic and revenues (which on the basis of UR's figures account for just over 70% of revenues) is reasonable, in our view; and there are arguments to support the reasonableness of the assumptions which have been adopted in preparing the forecasts. The UR report does not give a view on the expected margin of error of the forecasts of international passenger traffic and revenues. A qualitative estimate of reliability is that the forecasts are subject to a fair amount of uncertainty. Quantifying the margin of error would involve further work on sensitivity analysis. But it would be inappropriate, in our view, to delay a decision on the route in order to carry out further work on the forecasts, for two reasons. First, the additional information likely to be available in the short term appears unlikely to result in a material improvement in the reliability of the forecasts, although it may provide better information on the margin of error; and second, the time difference between alternative routes is small, such that the overall results are insensitive to the choice between routes.

(ii)    The approach to forecasting *domestic passenger* traffic and revenues has been a complex task, requiring the use of a number of forecasting models for different purposes at different stages of the analysis. In view of this, the approach is somewhat fragmented; but, in the time available, it is doubtful whether there was any practicable alternative available to Union Railways. Taking account of the constraints, the approach to domestic passenger traffic forecasting is reasonable, in our view. The UR report does not give a view on the expected margin of error of the domestic passenger revenue forecasts. They are subject to considerable uncertainty, but this should not affect the choice between routes.

(iii)    Union Railways estimate that the revenues from *freight* on CTRL will be very small. The forecasts of freight revenue are subject to a considerable degree of uncertainty, as UR acknowledges; but even if the forecasts were underestimated to a considerable extent, it should not affect the overall estimates or the choice between routes.

(iv)    Consultants appointed by the Department of the Environment have identified a considerable number of areas and sites likely to benefit substantially from CTRL. The location of development sites has been a major factor in Union Railways' consideration of detailed proposals for the route. Union Railways have not however been responsible for seeking to quantify the potential *development benefits*, and we have not therefore commented on the potential scale of such benefits.

**Investment appraisal**

15.    The conclusions on <u>investment appraisal</u> are as follows:

(i)    It appears to us that the appraisal carried out by Union Railways complies with the framework agreed with Government. The approach to the appraisal is broadly what we would expect. We consider that the UR team has put in place satisfactory procedures for checking the consistency, completeness and accuracy of the information used in the appraisal. The approach adopted by UR provides reasonable flexibility to test the effect of changes in the key assumptions. The appraisal makes some provision for taking account of future plans for BR.

(ii)    The results of the appraisal are clearly set out, showing the projected performance of the project in financial and cost/benefit terms.

(iii)    Sensitivity tests have been carried out by UR in accordance with procedures agreed with Government. These have not been carried out in combination (eg to test the combined effect of higher capital costs, a delay in the completion of construction and lower than expected revenues, or vice versa), but the framework for the appraisal did not require UR to do this.

(iv)    The appraisal does not lead to a preferred option and recommendations; but it has been agreed with Government that UR is not expected to make recommendations.

On the basis of these criteria, the approach to the investment appraisal is, in our view, reasonable.

## CHOICE OF REFERENCE CASE AND OPTIONS

### Introduction

16. The objective of this part of the study is to review the way in which Union Railways have optioneered the route to choose the reference case and options, and to assess whether the approach is reasonable. This part of the report is divided into two sections: (i) approach to optioneering the route; and (ii) assessment criteria and review.

### Approach to optioneering the route

17. Union Railways' brief from Government is set out in a letter from the Secretary of State for Transport to the Chairman of BR, dated 9 October 1991, the Department's paper *Developing the Route* of 20 October 1992 (both annexed to the UR report), and the Department's paper *Design Standards Brief* of May 1992. The brief requires Union Railways:

(i)     to identify a 'reference case route' based on the alignment which would maximise the financial return to the project before grant, taking into account both costs and revenues, while nevertheless meeting the environmental standards generally applied to other major transport infrastructure projects in this country, taking account of anticipated trends;

(ii)     in addition, where local variations would bring additional environmental or regeneration benefits, or greater benefits to commuters, to report on those options;

(iii)     in relation to stations and junctions, to find the strategy for the reference case route which brings the greatest financial return; and to develop options for stations and junctions on other routes so that these can be compared.

Additional requirements specified in the brief include the need to design the route as a two track passenger line with a potential freight capability, to have regard to the potential for promoting new development in acceptable locations, and to commission a risk assessment to look at the robustness of the cost and revenue forecasts, including an assessment of the timetable for construction. Further information on the brief is given in other documents issued by the Department, eg *Environmental Appraisal* of 20 October 1992 and *Moving Freight by Rail: Loading Gauge* of October 1992.

18. In addition, Union Railways has set its own key objectives for CTRL, in agreement with Government: (i) to provide the main railway link between Britain and continental Europe; (ii) to provide a major increase in capacity and improvement in quality of journeys between Kent and London; and (iii) to provide the transport spine for the East Thames Corridor development, shifting development pressure from the west to the east of London.

19. The process of optioneering the route to select the reference case and options is described in the UR report and can be summarised briefly as follows. Within the easterly approach corridor, various business strategies have been defined, including the necessary stations and junctions. A large data base for the corridor has been assembled. The route has been divided into five sections, and a large number of sub-route options within each section have been identified. To identify the best options, a process of successive <u>sifts</u> has been used, each sift being designed to stratify the options into more promising options to be

carried forward for further study and less promising options to be 'parked', ie not to be studied further unless more promising options proved to have unforeseen problems. At each sift, the options under consideration have been evaluated and ranked in terms of cost, business impact, environmental and planning effects, views expressed by local authority officers on a confidential basis, and possible effects on opportunities for development and regeneration. The more promising options in each section have been carried forward for more detailed assessment.

## Assessment criteria and review

### *Assessment criteria*

20. In considering whether Union Railways' approach to optioneering the route is reasonable, the following appear to us to be the principal criteria:

(i) Does Union Railways' work comply with the brief from Government?

(ii) Is the approach to route optioneering what one would expect in a project of this type, and has the work been carried out in a professional manner?

(iii) Have the reference case and options been developed in sufficient detail for the purpose of taking a decision about the route?

Union Railways' work is assessed briefly below against these criteria.

### *Does Union Railways' work comply with the brief from Government?*

21. The first question is whether the approach complies with the brief from Government. The first aspect of this is whether there is evidence to confirm that the reference case selected by Union Railways is the one which would maximise the financial return to the project while meeting the required environmental standards. (Compliance with environmental standards is covered later in this report.) The option selected as the reference case is the 'Board Reference Case'. The arguments put forward to show that this option meets the criteria for the reference case are: (i) A large number of route options have been identified and considered. (ii) Although options which have lower costs than the selected reference case have been identified, these have been rejected on grounds of non-compliance with environmental standards or planning considerations. We consider that there are reasonable grounds for concluding that the reference case meets the selection criteria east of Stratford, ie from Stratford to the Eurotunnel boundary at Cheriton (although of course there are other considerations which may affect whether the reference case is selected as the route to be taken forward for consultation). As noted above, BR has indicated that further work is in hand to examine the alignment of the route of CTRL between Stratford and the London terminal.

22. The brief requires Union Railways to report on options where local variations would bring additional environmental or regeneration benefits, or greater benefits to commuters. The UR report contains a range of options designed with this aim. For simplicity, however, this report deals mainly with the Board Reference Case. The brief also requires Union Railways to report on stations and junctions, including finding the strategy for the reference case route which brings the greatest financial return; and developing options for

stations and junctions on other routes so that these can be compared. The UR report identifies a number of possible options for stations on the new line and for connections to the existing railway network. Forecasts of additional revenue for station options are given in the UR report. The UR report suggests that it is not essential to make choices between all the possibilities at this stage, and that the scope for obtaining contributions from landowners and developers is likely to be maximised if the options are kept open at this stage, particularly for stations. We agree with this approach.

23.     The UR report does not contain a formal risk assessment covering the revenue forecasts or the construction programme, along the lines of the risk analysis of the capital costs. However, some assessment of risk on the revenues has been made using sensitivity analysis. In our view, the use of sensitivity analysis is an appropriate means of assessing risk provided that the key variables are correctly identified, the potential for variation of each of these is assessed, and the impact of such variation on the projected results is tested. The application of sensitivity analysis to the revenue forecasts is discussed later. There is a case for carrying out a risk assessment of the construction programme; it is understood that UR intends to carry out shortly an assessment of the risk of delay in the construction programme.

24.     On the basis of the information we have seen, we consider that Union Railways' work on choosing the reference case and options complies with the brief from Government.

### Has the work been carried out in a professional manner?

25.     The second question is whether the approach to route optioneering adopted by Union Railways is what one would expect in a project of this type, and whether the work has been carried out in a professional manner. The approach adopted, using a sequence of sifts, is one that is commonly used by engineers for route optioneering and may therefore be regarded as reasonable. In addition to reviewing the UR report and relevant working papers, we have attended successive sifts as observers. On the basis of the work we have seen, the approach to route development, and ultimately to the choice of different cases for evaluation, has been thorough, and we consider that the work has been carried out in a professional manner.

### Have the reference case and options been developed in sufficient detail?

26.     The third question is whether the reference case and options have been developed in sufficient detail for the purpose of taking a decision about the route. Some parts of the route have been developed to a slightly greater level of detail than others. However, on the basis of our Review, we consider that all parts east of Stratford have been developed to a level of detail which is sufficient for the purpose of taking a decision about the route.

## CAPITAL COSTS

### Introduction

27.    The objectives of this part of the Review are: (i) to establish whether reasonable assumptions have been made about the railway engineering requirements of the line; (ii) to establish whether appropriate measures to take account of safety considerations have been allowed for; (iii) to review the techniques used for estimating projected capital costs; (iv) to assess the level of reliability of the methods of estimation used, and indicate the margin of error; (v) to consider the reasonableness of the level of contingency or other allowances; (vi) to establish whether the capital costs are as robust as they can be expected to be, taking into account the stage of the work; and (vii) to confirm that the timetable for development and construction is reasonable, and that appropriate measures are being considered to minimise the risk of construction cost over-runs.

28.    We have reviewed these matters under four headings as follows: (i) railway engineering requirements, operations and safety; (ii) capital costs of the route and on-route stations (which reviews the techniques used, discusses the construction programme and gives a view on robustness); (iii) capital costs of the London terminal; and (iv) reliability of the estimates and risk analysis (covering matters relating to reliability, margins of error and contingencies).    Additional information is provided in Annex C on Railway Engineering Requirements, Annex D on the Basis of Preparation of the Capital Cost Estimates and Annex E on Reliability of the Capital Cost Estimates and Risk Analysis.    The grand total of the capital costs of the Board Reference Case is shown in the UR report to be of the order of £2,400 million.

### Railway engineering requirements, operations and safety

#### *Railway engineering standards*

29.    Union Railways have adopted provisional engineering standards for gauge, horizontal curvature, and gradients on CTRL.    The route is planned to be built to the large continental loading gauge UIC GB+, which will enable lorry trailers to be carried on freight wagons, and is the minimum required by the brief from Government.    The horizontal curvature standards adopted are designed to provide for stability and passenger comfort at high speed.    The normal maximum gradient standard adopted is, we consider, satisfactory for passenger trains.    The effect on freight operations is discussed below.    In our view, the engineering standards adopted by UR provide a satisfactory basis for alignment design.

30.    The UR team has also made assumptions about standards for tunnels on the route. An important assumption is whether to allow for single-track twin bore tunnels or twin-track single bore tunnels.    Other assumptions relate to the requirements for cross-passages between twin bores and the spacing of ventilation shafts.    We consider that UR's approach to tunnel design is reasonable.

*Freight capability*

31.    The brief from Government specifies that the route should be a two-track passenger line with a potential freight capability; the alignment must allow for freight traffic to be carried on the line, while not compromising the capability to carry passenger traffic fast and comfortably.  The UR report indicates that, on the basis of the gradient standards adopted, trains of more than a certain weight will require two locomotives for traction, which will result in additional operating costs.  However,  taking account of the expected volume of freight traffic, this is estimated by UR to be more economic than constructing flatter gradients.  Locations for passing loops have been identified, should the freight traffic justify their use, but the cost of providing loops has not been included in the capital cost estimates for the reference case.  Taking account of the low volume of freight traffic which is projected by UR to use the line, the approach to the provision of freight capability is, in our view, reasonable.

*Signalling*

32.    The signalling system is to be chosen at as late a stage as is reasonable, in order that advantage can be taken of improving technology.  This is a satisfactory policy, but the consequence is that signalling estimates are at risk.  However, the estimates amount to less than 5% of the total and have been addressed by the risk assessment.

*Railway operations*

33.    Outline timetables have been produced by UR to demonstrate that the line capacity exists for the operation of both domestic and international trains, with provision for freight train paths, allowing for the different speeds of each type of train.  The approach is reasonable, in our view.  Railway operations may need to be reviewed further when details of the London terminal are available.

*Safety*

34.    The UR report does not address safety considerations as a specific issue.  We have reviewed the work carried out by UR to take account of safety requirements.  In accordance with the normal procedure for new railway works, the safety requirements of the Railway Inspectorate and others are not stated definitely in advance of construction, as they evolve over time; rather, indications are given of what will be acceptable.  Final acceptance of the project is reserved for an inspection immediately before opening for passenger service, after construction expenditure has taken place.  There is thus a risk that costs will be incurred unnecessarily through over-provision, or that additional expenditure will need to be incurred in order to gain approval.  The UR team recognises this situation.  Assessment of safety risks is being carried out in a structured fashion, and the UR team intends to maintain the programme of discussions with the safety authorities.

## Capital costs of the route and on-route stations

35.   The estimates of capital costs for the route and on-route stations have been prepared by UR on the basis of assumptions about: (i) the contract strategy; (ii) the price base; (iii) the design adopted for the route and stations; and (iv) the project timescale (including the construction programme).  These are discussed below, and are described in more detail in Annex D.

### *Contract strategy*

36.   The term contract strategy is used here to cover the approach to procurement and tendering for construction; it includes procurement plans, the extent to which the design has been developed at the time of tendering for construction, the way in which the construction contract is managed, and the way in which risks are shared between the client and the contractor.

37.   The contract strategy for CTRL has yet to be determined.  Accordingly, the UR team has assumed, for the purposes of the report, that Union Railways will manage the design and will obtain detailed designs from consultants before letting construction contracts. UR's assumptions about contract strategy are conventional for Government investment in major civil engineering projects.  The conventional strategy involves procurement procedures and contractual risk-sharing, whereby certain risks would be carried by UR as the client.  The UR team has made no attempt to review alternative contract strategies or arrangements for development and implementation of the project.  Risks inherent in any other form of development or procurement have not been assessed.  As the brief from Government does not ask UR to consider options for contract strategy, the approach adopted by UR is reasonable, in our view.

### *Price base*

38.   The cost database used by the UR team was initiated for use in the earlier evaluation of the Southerly Approach, and all rates were expressed in prices current at that time, i.e. 2Q89.  The UR team has proposed that the rates and prices developed for this work should be used as the basis for the current estimates, expressed in 4Q92 prices.  This proposition is based on research into labour, plant and material cost levels over the period and is supported by published studies.  Reviews by authoritative sources, including government departments, indicate that tender price levels have declined between 2Q89 and 4Q92.  The UR team has judged that this trend cannot be sustained by the industry at large. They have taken the view that real costs are currently at a level equal to 2Q89 and these trends should be taken into account rather than the currently declining tender price trends.

39.   There is a risk in this assumption.  If 4Q92 tender price levels are indeed lower than 2Q89, then the base estimate will have a built in contingency.  An additional factor is the present concern by the authorities responsible for producing statistics that the current level of activity in the construction industry is at too low a level to produce valid samples for acceptable statistics to be produced.  The risk assessment makes a notional allowance for this risk.  A further important risk is the impact that such a large project will have on the construction market when tenders are sought.  The health of the overall market at the time may also pose a significant risk to price levels.  This risk could affect the reliability of the overall estimates but should not affect the choice between routes.

*Design of the route and on-route stations*

40.    The capital costs of the route and on-route stations comprise: (i) construction costs; (ii) project management costs; and (iii) property costs. The approach to the preparation of the capital cost estimates is described in Annex D. Design development allowances and general contingencies are excluded from these base estimates, and are considered in the associated risk study. The procedures and techniques adopted by the UR team to derive estimates are sound, in our view, and the work to date appears to have generally been carried out in accordance with them. It appears to us, from an examination of selected elements of the estimates, that the work has been executed in a professional manner and is at a level commensurate with the current stage of development of the design. We understand that the UR team is using a similar approach to the preparation of capital cost estimates in its further work on the alignment of the route of CTRL between Stratford and the London terminal.

*Project timescale and construction programme*

41.    The UR team has assumed an outline construction programme which allows completion of CTRL early in the year 2000. This programme takes account of tunnel driving needs, spoil disposal methods and construction work packaging.

42.    The construction programme contains the critical assumption that it will be possible to commit a certain level of funds and procure various work and supplies before Royal Assent (or approval under an alternative procedure) is obtained. This would include procurement of tunnel boring machines and commitment of significant advance works and enabling works. The UR team have estimated that the amount of these commitments prior to Royal Assent might approach 13% of the capital cost estimates for each case. The programme carries the risk that it may not be possible to commit the required level of funds and to procure the required works and supplies before Royal Assent; this could affect the overall costs, but should not affect the choice between routes.

## Capital costs of the London terminal

43.    The Kings Cross Project is not covered in the UR report. Although global figures are given in the UR report for the total cost of railway works at Kings Cross and an estimate of the proportion of the cost of the low level station which is attributable to the London terminal of CTRL, the report does not describe the basis of preparation of the estimate of the total cost of the railway works at Kings Cross or the method of apportioning the total cost between the low level station and other parts of the development. In preparing this report, therefore, we have not been able to comment on these costs, or any risks attached to them.

## Reliability of the estimates and risk analysis

44.    The base estimates produced for the various cases make no allowance for contingencies, design cost growth, unforeseen circumstances or other internal or external risks. The brief from Government requires UR to carry out a risk assessment to look at the robustness of the cost estimates, including an assessment of the timetable. The risk assessment is designed to predict a range of prices against a probability of achievement.

45.     The risk assessment involves estimating upper and lower limits for each type of cost.     We have conducted a high level review of the main risk areas of the project, both geographically and by engineering element.   On the basis of the information made available to us, it appears possible that, for some types of risk, (eg the impact of poor ground conditions on the cost of tunnelling and earthworks), the upper limit currently estimated could be exceeded.

46.     A margin of error in the range of -10% to +30% is normal for a project of this type at this stage of development.   This is the percentage spread which UR had considered before the introduction of the risk appraisal process.   The risk assessment approach adopted by UR indicates a range of -10% to +22% around the basic estimated capital cost of the Board Reference Case, within 95% confidence limits.   On the basis of our review, we do not consider that the margin of error of the estimated capital cost should be assumed to be less than the range of -10% to +30% which is normal for a project of this type at this stage of development.   This margin will need to be reviewed when detailed information on the London terminal and the construction programme is available.   UR's work so far does not include a risk appraisal of the construction programme; but we understand that the UR team intends shortly to carry out an assessment of the risk of delay in the construction programme.

## ENVIRONMENTAL IMPACT

### Introduction

47.    The objectives of this part of the study are: to review whether the approach taken in assessing the environmental impact of the reference case and the options is reasonable, and whether the projected impact is consistent with standards used for assessing the environmental effects of similar projects. This part of the report is divided into five sections: (i) standards for environmental assessment; (ii) approach; (iii) reasonableness of approach; (iv) consistency of approach with environmental standards; and (v) specific issues.

### Standards for environmental assessment

48.    In the Spring of 1992, the Government and Union Railways agreed that the environmental standards generally applied to other transport infrastructure projects in this country, taking account of anticipated trends, should form the basis of the reference case. There are currently no guidelines on environmental standards specifically written for railway development proposals.  However, railways are linear developments, like roads, and the Department published in 1983 the *Manual for Environmental Appraisals* ('MEA') for roads. Although this gives guidance on the methods to be used for environmental appraisal, it does not set specific environmental standards.  The MEA has been used by BR, and latterly by Union Railways, for developing the environmental appraisal methodology.

49.    In March 1992, the Standing Advisory Committee on Trunk Road Assessment published a new document *Assessing the Environmental Impact of Road Schemes* ('the SACTRA report').  The general tone of this report suggests a considerable advance in the standards of environmental assessment for road schemes over those proposed in the MEA. The possibility that environmental standards or the methods measuring effects may change is recognised in the SACTRA report by its suggestion that the environmental assessment manual, due out around the end of 1992, could be presented in a form where sections could be replaced from time to time as advice develops.  The SACTRA report further recommends that descriptions of mitigation measures should be widened to include the possibilities of preventing or off-setting a significant environmental effect as well as simply reducing it.  UR has taken on board SACTRA's advice, and incorporated the general tone of the report into its approach.

50.    Methods of evaluating environmental effects from linear development (with indications where appropriate UK or International standards may be used) are described in the paper prepared for the CIRIA publication entitled *Environmental Assessment: A Guide to the Identification, Evaluation and Mitigation of Environmental Issues in Construction Schemes*.  This paper was prepared by Environmental Resources Limited ('ERL'), UR's independent environmental consultant.

51.    In order to determine what standards should be used for assessment of environmental effects in specialist areas, and of overall effects, Union Railways have developed an Environmental Handbook, Volume 3 of which describes Environmental Design Aims for the CTRL project.  This is one of a series of documents developed by UR to ensure consistency of approach to environmental issues.  In addition, seminars have been held to discuss environmental standards being applied to major transportation infrastructure projects and which could be applied to CTRL.

52.     The UR team has attempted to anticipate standards which will apply when the Bill may be going through Parliament.  Predictions of environmental impact for the operational phase have been made for 15 years after opening of CTRL.  However, in accordance with Union Railways' brief, no attempt has been made to assess what standards will be in place at that time.  Given the pace of change of environmental standards at the moment, this is considered to be reasonable.

53.     During the environmental assessment and review process, ERL researched environmental standards applied to the planning, design and approval of other linear transport schemes both in the UK and Europe.  Their study revealed that there were no definite standards in the sense of unimpeachable rules and that no designations (except perhaps international sites) were automatically protected.  For the UK, it is apparent that more methods of mitigation are now being developed and employed.  There appears to be a tendency towards reducing effects on property and nuisance effects on residents, even if this means an increased effect on land-based resources.  Tunnelling is the only example of an environmental mitigation which would reduce the effect on land-based resources.  Impact on people versus impact on land-based resources is a choice which frequently has to be made in designing infrastructure projects.  There is currently no guidance on this issue.

**Approach to environmental assessment**

*Organisation*

54.     The Environment Department within Union Railways has two key roles.  One is environmental liaison, which is the provision of environmental information to other disciplines within the project regarding the sensitivity of environmental features and the severity of potential impacts.  It also liaises on environmental matters externally with various interested bodies.  The other key role is that of environmental assessment, which includes development of the Union Railways' environmental policy and management of the consultants' commissions to undertake environmental assessment and to produce an environmental statement for the project as required by the Regulations.

55.     Union Railways have appointed environmental consultants to carry out specialist studies in specific technical areas.  They have also appointed ERL to assist them in the direction of these studies and to prepare the Environmental Statement which will go forward with the Bill.  ERL have not undertaken any specialist studies; their role is to coordinate the output of the specialist environmental consultants and to assist Union Railways' Environment Department in auditing the data collected by the specialist consultants.  ERL's task has been to produce an overall environmental appraisal report of the full-length route options.  We support this approach.  The UR team has defined the work carried out up to the safeguarding of the route as 'Environmental Appraisal'.  Following the publication and safeguarding of the route, a full Environmental Assessment will be carried out, in accordance with the prevailing Regulations.

*Quality Assurance/audit trail*

56.     It appears that experience gained in the setting and development of environmental standards was not well recorded during early stages of the project (1989/90).  However,

within the UR Environment Department the audit trail is now very well defined, with proper procedures for validation of environmental data; the audit system is satisfactory, in our view.

*Methodology*

57.    Specific studies identify the receptors and resources likely to be affected, predict and quantify the potential operational impacts on those receptors and resources, evaluate the significance of the resulting effect, and identify further measures necessary to mitigate the effect.   In addition they assess the on-site and off-site construction activity impact of the proposed new railway in relation to each specialist area.   On site activities are defined as those occurring within the Limits of Land to be Acquired or Used ('LLAU') to construct the railway, while off-site activities are those occurring outside the LLAU.

58.    The environmental appraisal work is carried out in three stages - definition, development and appraisal.   These stages were agreed with the engineers as the best way to develop the project to take full account of both engineering and environmental aspects.   A simplified framework was used at the development stage, being a modified version of the full framework and designed to reflect the earliest stage of engineering development, ie the general lack of detailed information.   The simplified framework was completed by the engineering design team based upon sub-route options within each route section, and was validated by the specialist environmental assessment consultants ('EACs').   The full framework was applied to the sub-route options emerging after the second sift and was completed by the specialist EACs and validated by ERL.   This information was assembled for the full route options following the third sift and is acceptable, in our view.

59.    A key feature of the whole process was that the level of environmental input to the decision making process was consistent for all options and commensurate with the corresponding level of engineering detail.

60.    The base line data for the environmental studies is the Environmental Features Mapping, which is the computerised system recording designated areas.   During the course of the study from the first to the third sift, various appraisals were undertaken by the specialist EACs to expand this information.   All EACs were instructed to carry out reconnaissance level field work and in some cases had consultation with the relevant statutory bodies prior to the third sift.   Some EACs (eg those dealing with community aspects) were requested to do detailed surveys at specific locations where the need was identified and where public access was available.   The Environmental Features Mapping is now in place for the whole route and validation of the 4 km-wide route corridor is virtually complete.

61.    In order to reach a consensus on the environmental effect of a particular route, round table discussions were held with all specialist environmental consultants present, together with ERL and with the Union Railways Environment Department.   This is currently the only acceptable way to reach such a consensus of opinion.   It is important to have all environmental consultants present, even those who are not significantly concerned about the impact of a route for their particular specialist discipline.

62.    During the later stages of the route development process, changes of attitude sometimes arose as a result of site visits and discussions with external organisations or from perception of the elements through views of photomontages.   However, given the large number of options which were reviewed, we are satisfied that Union Railways have gone as

far as is practicable to minimise the risk of route options being wrongly parked for environmental reasons.

63.    Summary environmental information has been presented to officials at each sift. Following the third sift, ERL and the UR Environment Department reassessed all the effects and significance given to them by the specialist consultants, and rationalised a number of these to ensure consistency of approach by all consultants. These amendments were ratified by the EACs.

64.    Both the environmental sift and the integrated engineering and environmental sifts compared routes by assessing the merits or demerits of two similar engineering options and then comparing the two most favoured from such assessment. This is known as pairwise comparison and is in keeping with the MEA approach.

## Reasonableness of approach

65.    We consider that UR's approach has been reasonable, considering the difficulty of obtaining a consensus view of environmental impact. Guidelines have been developed for the assessment of effects and their ranking; views of environmental specialists have been assessed to ensure that the significance of one or more impacts has not been unreasonably magnified or under-stated; data validation has been comprehensive and independently carried out; and audit trails exist, recording all decisions made. It is reasonable to consider both current environmental standards and those which may apply at some time in the future when the railway is operating - both these aspects have been addressed by the UR team.

66.    The environmental appraisal is based on a passenger railway, and does not include freight considerations. Specific aspects related to the use of freight trains are the need for passing loops and the different qualities of noise and vibration generated by these trains compared to those generated by high speed passenger trains. Given the level of detail at which this appraisal has been undertaken, we believe that consideration of these aspects would not have materially affected the outcome. It is understood that a preliminary appraisal has been carried out on passing loops.

## Consistency with environmental standards

67.    There are no specific standards for assessing the environmental impact of a railway development. Union Railways, through ERL, have made strenuous efforts to determine and apply standards which are consistent with those used on other major transport infrastructure projects and to examine the precedents for adhering to given standards. They have found that there are no specific standards and that environmental designations are not automatically protected. They have sought to minimise the effects on people, to avoid demolition, minimise landtake and to avoid internationally designated sites.

## Specific issues

### *Public consultation*

68.    Union Railways have carried out consultation with local authorities and statutory consultees to evaluate the issues of local concern. These have been taken into account in the evaluation of the options at the various sifts. Until the public (including local environmental

groups) have been consulted on the route, there will always be a possibility that choices made in the selection of options will be revised once the route is published, but this is a normal feature of the planning process.

### *Effect of exaggerating environmental significance*

69.    At the environmental round table discussions there have been some differences of opinion as to the magnitude of an effect as expressed by some of the environmental consultants.  These have been quite marked in some instances, but ERL, in their regulating role, have reviewed all decisions made to minimise any over- or under-statement.  ERL's amendments have been agreed by the EACs.

### *Construction through landfill*

70.    Concern has been expressed in relation to construction through landfill sites.  This is principally because of the nature of the fill material, which may result in excessive settlement which would be unacceptable for a high speed railway, the potentially aggressive nature of the materials within or migrating from the fill material and the general procedural difficulties of dealing with rigorously controlled hazardous substances such as gas and leachate.  The route has generally been engineered to avoid landfill sites and where this has not been possible, construction costs make allowance for piling and for removal of waste materials or other measures necessary to ensure that the track is not constructed over or through waste.

### *Toxic freight*

71.    Discussions between UR and the National Rivers Authority ('NRA') have resulted in agreement that 'blanket' sealing of the track over areas designated Aquifer Protection Zone 1 is not required.  However, the NRA has indicated that for specific sections of route which run close to sensitive abstraction points, there may be a need to seal the track formation.  The UR team considers that the cost of meeting the NRA's eventual requirements can be accommodated within the general provisions already made for route construction.

### *Costs/environment trade off*

72.    The process of optioneering has ensured that options which do not meet the environmental standards required have been parked and have not been presented to Government.  The options presented thus comprise those where environmental effects may be considered acceptable or where mitigation can reduce adverse environmental effects to an acceptable level, with only moderate increases in cost.  Where possible, mitigation has been incorporated through minor changes to alignment and the cost implications are thus included in the engineering costs for each option.  Items in the cost build-up allow for the provision of additional concessions in certain areas known still to be sensitive, and we believe that the sums set aside are reasonable.  The cost of 'bolt-on' mitigation is included in general engineering costs and covers retaining walls, planting and noise barriers.  We are satisfied with UR's approach to the inclusion of environmental mitigation measures and the evaluation of their costs.

# TRAFFIC AND REVENUE FORECASTS

## Introduction

73.     The terms of reference set the following objectives for the review of traffic and revenue forecasts: (i) to review the techniques used for preparing the forecasts; (ii) to assess whether the assumptions and forecasts are reasonable; (iii) to confirm that appropriate measures have been taken by UR to ensure that the forecasts are consistent with relevant agreements such as the Revenue Sharing Agreement between BR, SNCF and SNCB ('the Railways'); (iv) to review the forecasts of operating costs, and assess whether they are reasonable; and (v) to indicate the possible margins of error of the forecasts.

74.     This part of the report is divided into four sections covering: (i) *international passenger* traffic and revenues (including operating costs); (ii) *domestic passenger* traffic and revenues (including operating costs); (iii) *freight* revenues; and (iv) *development* benefits. The reliability of the estimates is covered in the individual sections.  International passenger revenues (which on the basis of UR's figures account for just over 70% of revenues) are covered in more detail than domestic passenger revenues (which account for around 20% of revenues) and freight revenues.  In line with the terms of reference, this part focuses on the forecasts of revenues, and does not review the estimates of non-financial benefits to users or non-users.  As agreed with the Department, the forecasts are based on the present regime for track access; no account has been taken, at this stage, of potential changes arising from open access.

## International passenger traffic and revenues

### *Techniques used*

75.     The principal techniques used in the preparation of the current forecasts of international passenger traffic and revenue can be summarised broadly as follows.  Estimates have been prepared of the size and growth rate of the total market for trips between Britain and France, Benelux and Germany by all modes of travel.  Assumptions have been made about the Railways' fare structure and average fares.  An assessment has then been made of the share of the total market which would be captured by the Railways, taking account of rail's competitive position (eg comparative travel time and cost) against other modes, and an estimate of the extent of any additional traffic generated by CTRL.  The gross revenues earned by the Railways has then been calculated, together with BR's share of the gross revenue, taking account of the Revenue Sharing Agreement.  BR's net revenue has then been calculated, after deduction of operating costs.  Estimates have also been made of the revenue-earning potential of individual stations.

76.     The techniques used for the preparation of the current forecasts of international passenger traffic and revenues represent further development of techniques which have been developed by BR and its advisers over a number of years for preparing forecasts of international passenger traffic.  The development of these techniques was described in the report *Rail Link Project: Comparison of traffic, revenues and benefits* prepared by Coopers & Lybrand and published by BR in May 1991.  The emphasis of recent work, in addition to updating the forecasts, has been to focus on the terminal or station which travellers would use.  The techniques used by Union Railways both build on the previous work and are also broadly in line with the techniques which we would expect to be used for the preparation of

forecasts of traffic and revenues. On this basis, it appears to us that the techniques used are reasonable.

### Assumptions and forecasts

77. It appears to us that the principal assumptions (or sets of assumptions) used in preparing the forecasts of international passenger traffic and revenue are as follows:

(i)     the size of the total market and its rate of growth;

(ii)    journey times to the Channel Tunnel (with and without CTRL);

(iii)   fare structure and average fares;

(iv)    the level of services to be offered;

(v)     the Railways' market share (with and without CTRL); and

(vi)    BR's share of the total revenue earned by the Railways.

78. We asked Union Railways what evidence there was to support the reasonableness of the above assumptions. We also asked what steps had been taken to ensure that the traffic and revenue forecasts were up-to-date and based on the latest available information; and, if any aspect of the forecasts was based on information which had not been updated recently, what evidence there was to suggest that the use of older data would not materially affect the reliability of the forecasts. The answers are discussed in the following sections, where appropriate.

### The total market

79. The first set of assumptions relates to the size and rate of growth of the total market for trips between Britain and France, Benelux and Germany by all modes of travel. We asked Union Railways what action they had taken to confirm the reasonableness of the assumptions about the size and growth rate of the total market. They informed us that they had commissioned the Henley Centre for Forecasting to advise on the size and future growth rates of the international market, taking account of the latest available information. They indicated that the assumptions which they adopted were broadly consistent with the advice received from the Henley Centre. This appears to us to be a reasonable approach.

### Journey times to the Channel Tunnel with and without CTRL

80. The second set of assumptions relates to journey times to the Channel Tunnel with and without CTRL. These assumptions are used in assessing the competitive position of international rail services against other modes. The assumptions adopted by UR about journey time savings projected to arise from CTRL are set out clearly in the UR report.

### Fare structure and average fares

81. The assumptions about fare structure are based on comparison with competing modes, notably air and coach; for example business fares in the period before CTRL opens

are set at a level which is designed to compete with air fares, taking account of expected reductions in air fares resulting from liberalisation in the single European market. It is assumed that there is a price increase when CTRL opens. We understand that EPS has received independent advice on fares. Taking account of this, the approach taken is, in our view, reasonable.

*Level of services to be offered*

82.    The assumptions about the level of services to be offered and their relationship to the demand forecasts are not given in any detail in the UR report. We asked Union Railways whether there would be sufficient capacity on international services to cope satisfactorily with the forecast level of traffic at peak times. Union Railways indicated that: the forecasts take account of some excess of demand over capacity at peak times in the peak period; and the fare structure, incorporating higher fares at peak times, is designed to encourage travellers to avoid the peaks. We have no evidence to suggest that this approach is inappropriate.

*The Railways' market share (with and without CTRL)*

83.    The forecast of the Railways' share of the total international market is calculated using a model which allocates the Railways' share of the total market based on the attractiveness of through rail services compared with other modes. Through rail services are effectively a new mode of travel in this market and there is no data on the actual preferences of travellers. Although some market research is available, an element of judgement has to be used in estimating its market share. Union Railways have informed us that they do not expect to have a clear picture of the relative attractiveness of through rail services versus other modes until the Channel Tunnel has opened and the traffic patterns have settled down, say in 1995. In forecasting the growth in traffic with CTRL, Union Railways have assumed that some traffic will be captured from other modes and some will be new (generated) traffic. We understand that the estimate of generated traffic is based on an assumption about the volume of generated traffic taken from BR Passenger Forecasting Handbook. The approach to forecasting the Railways' market share appears reasonable; in interpreting the results, account needs to be taken of the extent to which judgement has been used in assessing how passengers will assess the attractiveness of through rail services against competing modes.

84.    The forecasts of market share depend to some extent on information which is not up-to-date. Some of the information used in this work is based on data from the 1985/86 International Passenger Survey ('IPS'), which contained special questions designed to elicit information about modal choice. In 1991 this survey was carried out containing similar questions to those asked in 1985/86, but analysis of these results was not available in time for incorporation in UR's work. We asked Union Railways what evidence there was to support the view that the use of 1985/86 data would not materially reduce the reliability of the forecasts. They indicated that the principal benefit of the information in the new survey would be for comparing the relative merits of different service patterns, rather than in estimating the size and growth of the total market. On that basis, the UR team considered that it was not essential to wait for the new IPS information, expected early in 1993. We agree with the UR team's view.

*BR's share of total revenue*

85. BR's share of the total revenue earned by the Railways is determined by the Revenue Sharing Agreement. For reasons of confidentiality, access to the agreement is restricted to a small number of BR personnel. We have confirmed that appropriate measures have been taken to check that the forecasts are consistent with relevant agreements (eg the Revenue Sharing Agreement with SNCF and SNCB); the calculations of BR's share of the Railways' revenue have been prepared by EPS and checked by Union Railways for consistency with the Revenue Sharing Agreement. This is acceptable, in our view.

## *Operating costs*

86. Operating costs for international passenger services have been developed by EPS as part of their business plan projections. Since EPS services are not yet operating, these costs will be more uncertain than those for domestic services. The approach taken by EPS to the preparation of projections of operating costs is broadly what we would expect; we have not reviewed the forecasts in detail.

## *Reliability*

87. The UR team has not carried out a formal risk assessment on the revenue forecasts along the lines of the risk analysis undertaken on the capital costs. Some sensitivity tests have been carried out by UR on the forecasts, looking at the effects of higher or lower demand growth and higher or lower air fares. The UR report does not, on the basis of these tests, give a view on the expected margin of error of the international passenger revenue forecasts. A qualitative estimate of reliability is that the forecasts of international passenger traffic and revenues are subject to a fair amount of uncertainty, for a number of reasons (such as the difficulty of forecasting how passengers will assess the attractiveness of rail services through the Channel Tunnel, when it opens, against competing modes). Quantifying the margin of error would involve further work on sensitivity analysis, to identify all the key variables, to assess the potential for variation of each of these, and to test the impact of such variation on the projected results. But it would be inappropriate, in our view, to delay a decision on the route in order to carry out further work on the forecasts, for two reasons. First, the additional information likely to be available in the short term appears unlikely to result in a material improvement in the reliability of the forecasts, although it may provide better information on the margin of error; and second, the time difference between alternative routes is small, such that the overall results are insensitive to the choice between routes.

## Domestic passenger traffic and revenues

### *Techniques, assumptions and forecasts*

88. Following the comparative evaluation exercise in 1990-91, Union Railways have developed their approach to domestic traffic forecasting. This has relied on a number of forecasting models applied to different stages of the analysis and for different purposes. Individually, all items of user and non-user cost/benefit appear to be addressed. The models use recognised and accepted techniques. In view of the limitations of some of the existing models, a new domestic forecasting model has been developed to provide forecasts more quickly. The use of a number of different models means that the approach to domestic traffic

forecasting is somewhat fragmented; but, in the time available, it is doubtful whether there was any practicable alternative available to Union Railways.

89. The forecasts of domestic traffic are subject to a number of limitations. The interaction between transport demand and land use could not be incorporated into the overall approach; no estimate has been made of the disbenefits that will be caused to existing passenger and freight services as a result of disruption during construction of the high speed line (although some allowance has been made for the cost of measures to minimise such disruption); and a large amount of judgement has been needed in developing the forecasting techniques and assumptions. These considerations need to be taken into account in interpreting the forecasts.

*Operating costs*

90. Forecasts of operating costs for domestic services have been prepared by NSE. The approach taken by NSE to the preparation of these forecasts is broadly what we would expect; we have not reviewed the forecasts in detail.

*Reliability*

91. Similar considerations apply to the reliability of the domestic passenger forecasts as to the international passenger forecasts. The UR report does not give a view on the expected margin of error of the domestic passenger revenue forecasts. Quantification of the margin of error would involve further work on sensitivity analysis. The forecasts of domestic traffic and revenues are subject to considerable uncertainty, but this should not in our view affect the choice between routes.

**Freight revenues**

92. The amount of freight revenues included in the analysis is relatively small. This reflects the level of freight traffic which has been forecast and the assumption that freight traffic will generally travel on existing routes to the Channel Tunnel rather than the CTRL. We have not reviewed the freight forecasts in detail.

93. No quantified estimate of the margin of error on freight revenues is available. The forecasts of freight revenue have been the subject of an independent review by a firm of transport consultants, which concluded that they were probably of the right order, although subject to a considerable degree of uncertainty. But even if the forecasts were underestimated to a considerable extent, it should not in our view affect the overall estimates or the choice between routes.

**Development benefits**

94. Consultants appointed by the Department of the Environment have identified a considerable number of areas and sites likely to benefit substantially from CTRL. The location of development sites has been a major factor in Union Railways' consideration of detailed proposals for the route. Union Railways have not however been responsible for seeking to quantify the potential *development benefits*, and we have not therefore commented on the potential scale of such benefits.

# INVESTMENT APPRAISAL

## Introduction

95. The objective of this part of the study is to review the way in which Union Railways has carried out the investment appraisal, and to assess whether the approach is reasonable. The investment appraisal is given in Chapter 13 of the UR report; further information is given in working papers. These documents provide summary cash flow projections for the project in terms of net present values and internal rates of return, and detailed cash flow projections. This part of the report is divided into two sections: (i) approach to the appraisal; and (ii) assessment of the approach.

## Approach to the appraisal

96. The approach to the appraisal has been based on a framework developed and agreed through discussions between Union Railways and the Department, and is described in the UR report. It involves different *levels of analysis* (eg financial level, financial plus benefits from domestic traffic etc), different *cases* (eg Board Reference Case, Board Policy Case), different *standards of environmental mitigation*, different *bases* (eg whole business basis, incremental basis), different *discount rates*, a risk assessment, and a range of sensitivity tests. The approach is based, in part, on the framework of analysis developed for the comparison of routes in 1991.

## Assessment of the approach

97. In considering whether the approach to the appraisal is reasonable, we have used the following principal criteria:

(i) Compliance with the agreed framework. Does the appraisal comply with the framework agreed with Government?

(ii) Consistency, completeness and accuracy. Has the information used in the appraisal been prepared on a consistent basis? Is the information complete? Have the results been correctly calculated on the basis of the assumptions stated?

(iii) Flexibility. Does the way in which the appraisal has been designed provide flexibility to assess the effect on the results of making changes in the key assumptions?

(iv) Compatibility with future plans for BR. Does the approach take account (as far as it is possible to do so) of future plans for BR?

(v) Are the results clearly presented in a way which is consistent with good practice?

These are considered in the following paragraphs.

*Does the approach comply with the agreed framework?*

98.    The first question is whether the appraisal complies with the framework agreed with Government.  It appears to us that the analysis carried out by Union Railways complies with the framework described above.  It provides different levels of analysis, different cases, different standards of environmental mitigation, different bases, different discount rates, a risk assessment, and a range of sensitivity tests, as required by the brief.

*Is the information consistent, complete and accurate?*

99.    We asked Union Railways what steps they had taken to ensure that the information had been prepared on a consistent basis, was complete, and had been correctly calculated on the basis of the assumptions stated.  Union Railways indicated that instructions had been issued to all concerned, designed to ensure that the figures were prepared on a consistent basis.  We have reviewed these instructions.  UR also commissioned their own review of the international and domestic forecasts.  On completeness, they indicated that the information obtained from various sources for use in the appraisal had been reviewed within the appraisal team to ensure that there were no material omissions.  They stated that in their view there were no material exclusions which should be drawn to Government's attention.  We are satisfied with the information and explanations provided by UR.

*Does the approach provide flexibility to assess the effect of changes?*

100.    The next question is whether the way in which the appraisal has been designed provides flexibility to assess the effect on the results of making changes in the key assumptions.  For example, if a design change is made which reduces capital costs but increases operating costs, does the appraisal process enable the effect of changing the assumptions to be calculated automatically?  We understand that this depends on the nature of changes which are made.  A number of models have been used for the appraisal process, and the interface between some of these is manual.  The effect of a change may therefore be incorporated automatically in one model, but if the results are then passed to a second model, the results may have to be transferred manually.  In some cases (for example the effect on operating costs of using steeper gradients), Union Railways judged that the effects were minimal, and no adjustment was made.  We accept this explanation.

*Does the approach take account of future plans for BR?*

101.    The next question is whether account has been taken of future plans for BR. Consideration has been given by Union Railways to the feasibility of taking account of future plans for BR, for example the introduction of charges for access to track and other infrastructure.  However, information on the details of possible track charges has not been available for inclusion in the appraisal.  Provision has therefore been made in the appraisal for incorporating such charges as and when information becomes available.  We consider that this approach is reasonable in the circumstances.

### *Are the results clearly presented in a way consistent with good practice?*

102. The results of the appraisal are clearly set out. The appraisal is not described in detail in the UR report, but it is made clear that the presentation is intended as a broad guide to the financial position of the project rather than a detailed investment appraisal. As is indicated, the overall findings are based on a substantial amount of detailed analysis, which is recorded in working papers.

103. The projected performance of the project (in financial and cost/benefit terms) is expressed in terms of internal rates of return, together with calculations of net present value at the alternative discount rates. The approach is in line with the brief and with normal practice in investment appraisal.

104. Sensitivity tests (to show the effect of a change in one of the key assumptions on the internal rate of return or net present value of the project) have been carried out by UR in accordance with a list of tests agreed with Government, and have been reported. These tests generally involve testing the effect of a change in a single assumption. The tests shown do not include tests of combinations of assumptions (eg to test the combined effect of higher capital costs, a delay in the completion of construction and lower than expected revenues, or vice versa). However, the framework for the appraisal did not require UR to do this.

105. The appraisal does not lead to a preferred option and recommendations, as is commonly the case at the conclusion of an investment appraisal. However, the absence of recommendations is consistent with UR's stated intentions and the agreed approach to the appraisal.

Samuel Montagu & Co. Limited
WS Atkins Planning Consultants
March 1993

# ANNEX A: GLOSSARY

| | |
|---|---|
| Base case | The 'do minimum' case, including Phases 1 & 2 of EPS but not CTRL |
| Board Reference Case | The route alignment selected by BR as the reference case |
| Easterly route | Route corridor based on the conceptual alignment proposed by Ove Arup, approaching London from the East via Stratford |
| Environmental standards | The environmental standards generally applied to other major transport infrastructure projects in this country, taking account of anticipated trends |
| Investment appraisal | A systematic approach to expenditure decisions; it entails deciding clearly the objectives of an expenditure proposal, considering the various ways of meeting them and working out and presenting the costs and benefits of each option |
| Optioneering | The process of identifying superior route options through a process of successive sifts |
| Parked (option) | A route option which has been judged inferior to other options at a sift and which will not be studied further unless more promising options prove to have unforeseen consequences |
| Property costs | Costs of acquiring property needed for the defined permanent works and construction sites, together with allowances for disturbance and demolition |
| Reference case | The route alignment which is designed to maximise the financial return to the CTRL project, taking into account both costs and revenues, while nevertheless meeting the environmental standards |
| Risk analysis or risk assessment | Process designed to predict a range of costs (or revenues) against a probability of achievement.  It is designed to replace the addition of percentage allowances for contingencies |
| Sift | The process undertaken several times whereby more promising options are selected for further study and less promising options are parked |
| Southerly Approach | Alignment evaluated previously, which approached London from the South via Swanley |

# ANNEX B: TERMS OF REFERENCE FOR THE INDEPENDENT REVIEW OF CTRL

**Purpose of the review**

1.   The purpose of the review is to provide the Department with an independent assessment of whether the work by BR on the preparation of the reference case and options for the Channel Tunnel Rail Link on the easterly route has been carried out in a reasonable way.  The review will address the issues at a strategic level and is not intended to duplicate the work of BR's Rail Link Project (RLP) team.

**Scope of the review**

2.   The review is expected to cover the following areas:

i)  **reference case and options**

-   to review the method by which BR has chosen the reference case and options, and to assess whether the approach is reasonable;

ii)  **capital costs**

-   to review the techniques used for estimating projected capital costs;
-   to assess the level of reliability of the methods of estimation used, and indicate the margin of error;
-   to consider the reasonableness of the level of contingency or other allowances;
-   to establish that the capital costs are as robust as they can be expected to be at this stage of the work;
-   to confirm that the timetable for development and construction is reasonable and that appropriate measures are being considered to minimise the risk of construction cost overrun;

iii)  **railway engineering and operations**

-   to establish that reasonable assumptions have been made about the railway engineering requirements of the line;
-   to establish that appropriate measures to take account of safety considerations have been allowed for;
-   to review the basis of preparation of the projected railway operating costs, and assess whether the projected operating costs are reasonable, and to indicate the margin of error;

iv)  **traffic and revenue forecasts**

-   to review the techniques used for estimating traffic and revenue forecasts;
-   to assess whether the assumptions and forecasts are reasonable;
-   to indicate the possible margin of error;
-   to confirm that appropriate measures have been taken by BR to ensure that the forecasts are consistent with relevant agreements (eg the revenue sharing agreement with SNCF and SNCB);

v)  **environmental impact**

-   to review whether the approach taken to assessing the environmental impact of the reference case and the options is reasonable, and whether the projected impact is consistent with environmental standards.

3 June 1992

## ANNEX C: RAILWAY ENGINEERING REQUIREMENTS, OPERATIONS AND SAFETY

**Railway engineering standards**

1.      The railway engineering standards have been developed by UR during the course of the work.  They have been issued with provisional status for route alignment determination. They are based on BR practice, amended to suit high speed operation.  The key standards at this route definition stage are geometric:

(i)      High speed trains require large radius horizontal alignments for stability and passenger comfort.  Minimum horizontal curvature is determined by reference to the speed of international passenger trains, the applied cant and acceptable cant deficiency.   The maximum cant of 150mm being adopted by UR may cause rail and wheel wear for slow speed freight trains, but this is not a significant factor.

(ii)     Greater clearances between passing trains and between trains and structures are required to mitigate the aerodynamic effects created by higher speed and to provide higher safety levels, so a wider track bed is required than for existing BR trains.

(iii)    Steeper gradients can be used for passenger railways, compared with heavy freight, owing to the greater power of the vehicles and the increased momentum at high speed.  The effect on freight operations is discussed below.  Gradient standards have been changed during the route development process; gradients up to 2½% (1 in 40) are currently being used, which is considered satisfactory for passenger vehicles.  This has a significant effect in reducing earthworks volumes and tunnel lengths, and thus construction costs.

(iv)     The route is planned to be built to the large continental loading gauge UIC GB+, which will enable lorry trailers to be carried on freight wagons and is the minimum required by the brief from Government.  Larger loading gauges, eg UIC C, have been considered, but there are a number of arguments against them, eg they would be inconsistent with French Railways' existing line to the Channel Tunnel, which is being upgraded to UIC B+.

In our view, the standards provide a satisfactory basis for alignment design.

**Freight capability**

2.      While it has not been designed specifically for freight, the line is capable of being used by freight trains.  Trains of more than a certain weight (which might be of the order of 1,000 tonnes) will require two locomotives for traction, owing to the relatively steep gradients, which will be inconvenient and will increase operating costs, but this should be less costly than constructing flatter gradients for the expected volume of freight traffic. Locations for passing loops have been identified, should the freight traffic justify their use, but the cost of providing loops has not been included in the capital cost estimates.  In our view, this approach is reasonable, given the  low freight volumes anticipated by UR.

## Signalling

3.      The signalling system is to be chosen at as late a stage as is reasonable, in order that advantage can be taken of improving technology.   This is a satisfactory policy, but its consequence is that signalling estimates are at risk.   The estimates amount to less than 5% of the total and have been addressed by the risk assessment.   They are based on a number of recently completed and proposed BR projects and will be subject to adjustment as the definition of signalling requirements is developed.

## Railway operations

4.      The EPS Business Plan, covering the operation of international passenger services in the period from the opening of the Channel Tunnel, is based on the use of existing tracks and London Waterloo, rather than the CTRL.   The operating costs shown in the plan are not therefore relevant to operations on CTRL.   NSE costs assume a rolling stock fleet broadly in line with the March 1992 paper by NSE *Network Rolling Stock: Fleet Strategy to 2005*, with adjustments for the 1992 NSE Commuter Forecasts and agreed assumptions for major projects, real pricing and quality standards.   Energy and maintenance costs for rolling stock are assumed to be equivalent for all types of vehicle, based on experience of the class 317. No additional services have been assumed; rather, it has been assumed that additional capacity can be achieved by use of maximum train lengths.   No commissioning costs for the rolling stock have been identified as the stock will have been in service for some time before CTRL opens.

5.      We have been shown outline timetables produced by UR to demonstrate that the line capacity exists for both domestic and international trains, with provision for freight train paths.   The different speeds of each type of train are allowed for.   Crossovers every 5km, and 2-way signalling, are allowed to cater for emergencies.   The approach is reasonable, in our view.   Railway operations may need to be reviewed further when details of the London terminal are available.

## Safety

6.      Assessment of safety risks is being carried out in a structured fashion.   In accordance with the normal procedure for new railway works, the safety requirements of the Railway Inspectorate and others are not stated definitely in advance of construction, as they evolve over time; rather, indications are given of what will be acceptable.   Final acceptability of the project is reserved for an inspection immediately before opening for passenger service, when construction expenditure has taken place.   There is thus a risk that costs will be incurred unnecessarily, through over-provision, or that additional costs will need to be incurred for remedial works required to gain approval.   The UR team recognises this situation, and intends to maintain the programme of discussions with the safety authorities. We expect UR to present the safety case at key stages of the project in order to obtain interim approvals from BR and the Railway Inspectorate.

7.      With regard to numerical safety estimates (based on probabilistic assessment), advanced discussions have taken place between BR and the Health and Safety Executive ('HSE'), but acceptance by the Railway Inspectorate division of the HSE of numerical rather than judgemental assessment has not yet been agreed.   We consider that staged agreement to the safety case and an agreed basis for numerical assessment could substantially reduce the

risk of late design changes, such as led to significant cost increases and delays for Eurotunnel.

8.     One area in particular where safety requirements might have significant construction effects is the safety case for twin-bore tunnels against two tracks in a single bore.  This needs to be discussed with the Railway Inspectorate.  Twin bore is generally considered safer than single bore in that one bore provides a place of safety from a fire or accident occurring in the other; subsidence is also likely to be less, but over a wider area.  In the North Downs and the Thames Crossing tunnels, single bore construction is substantially cheaper owing to the chalk tunnelling strata, but this is not the case for London tunnels.  The North Downs tunnel is assumed as single bore, twin track and thus there is a risk that the Railway Inspectorate will require twin bores.  The tunnel beneath the Thames is also proposed to be constructed as twin bore to allow acceptable gradients, given UR's current knowledge of the river bed.  This will be reviewed when site investigation data are available. If twin bores are required on all tunnels it is expected to add between 3 and 4 % to UR's cost estimates for cases which have extensive lengths in tunnel, but less than 1% of the estimates for the Board Reference and Policy cases.  The requirements for cross passages between twin bores should also be reviewed with the Railway Inspectorate to determine the maximum acceptable spacing.  We consider that UR's approach to tunnel design is reasonable; however it should be noted that UR recognise this as a risk area and intend to carry out stringent reviews of their proposed tunnelling methodology before award of construction contracts.

9.     Ventilation shafts for long tunnels are assumed at approximately 3 km intervals. Each contains 2 draught relief shafts and 1 access shaft.  The spacing is that determined for the Southerly Approach and is related to pressure relief, smoke extraction and passenger comfort (the ambient temperature for air conditioning operation).  These assumptions are reasonable, in our view; any change to shaft spacing would require reassessment of all these factors.

WSA

## ANNEX D: BASIS OF PREPARATION OF THE CAPITAL COST ESTIMATES

### Introduction

1.    The estimates of capital costs for the route and on-route stations are prepared on the basis of assumptions about: (i) contract strategy; (ii) the price base; (iii) the design adopted for the route and stations; and (iv) the project timescale and construction programme.  These are discussed below.

### Contract strategy

2.    The term contract strategy is used here to cover the approach to procurement and tendering for construction; it includes procurement plans, the extent to which the design has been developed at the time of tendering for construction, the way in which the construction contract is managed, and the way in which risks are shared between the client and the contractor.

3.    The contract strategy for CTRL has yet to be determined.  Accordingly, the UR team has assumed, for the purposes of the report, that Union Railways will manage the design and will obtain detailed designs from consultants before letting construction contracts.  UR's assumptions about contract strategy are conventional for Government investment in major civil engineering projects.  On the basis of these assumptions, UR would be the client; a fully developed design would exist at the time of tendering for construction; and construction contracts would be let on the basis that UR as the client would take the financial risks on the sufficiency of the design and the quantification of the work.  Construction work would be supervised by engineers appointed by UR.  The conventional strategy involves procurement procedures and contractual risk-sharing, whereby certain risks would be carried by UR as the client.  The UR team has made no attempt to review alternative contract strategies or arrangements for development and implementation of the project.  Risks inherent in any other form of development or procurement have not been assessed.  As the brief does not ask UR to consider options for contract strategy, the approach adopted by UR is reasonable, in our view.

### Price base

4.    The cost database used by the UR team was initiated for use in the earlier evaluation of the Southerly Approach, and all rates were expressed in prices current at that time, i.e. 2Q89.  The UR team has proposed that the rates and prices developed for this work should be used as the basis for the current estimates, expressed in 4Q92 prices.  This proposition is based on research into labour, plant and material cost levels over the period and is supported by published studies.  The 1989 estimates were estimates of tender prices which assumed that the client would take the risk of future cost escalation during design and construction.  Reviews by authoritative sources, including government departments, indicate that tender price levels have declined between 2Q89 and 4Q92.  The UR team has judged that this trend cannot be sustained by the industry at large.  They have taken the view that as real costs are currently at a level equal to 2Q89 these trends should be taken into account rather than the currently declining tender price trends.

5.      There is a risk in this assumption.  If 4Q92 tender price levels are indeed lower than 2Q89, then the base estimate will have a built in contingency.  An additional factor is the present concern by the authorities responsible for producing statistics that the current level of activity in the construction industry is at too low a level to produce valid samples for acceptable statistics to be produced.  A further important risk is the impact that such a large project will have on the construction market when tenders are sought.  The health of the overall market at the time may also pose a significant risk to price levels.

**Design of the route and on-route stations**

6.      The estimates of the capital costs of the route and on-route stations comprise: (i) construction costs; (ii) project management costs; and (iii) property costs.   Design development allowances and general contingencies are excluded from these base estimates, and are considered in the associated risk study.  The capital costs have been prepared on the basis that CTRL represents an increment to BR's existing activities; the capital costs of the route and on-route stations therefore exclude the capital costs of these existing activities. Examples of cost headings excluded are: (i) Phases I & II costs (eg Waterloo International Terminal, Ashford International Passenger Station, the maintenance depot at North Pole, the freight depot at Dollands Moor and other off-line works); these costs relate to the whole business evaluation; (ii) UR team management costs to date; (iii) cost of property purchased to date along the  redundant Southerly Approach; (iv) design development allowances and general contingencies, which are computed separately following the associated risk study; (v) provision for an on-route station at Stratford; (the costs of this would be additional); and (vi) any increases in estimated construction costs beyond 4Q92 as a result of inflation of resources costs and/or change in market conditions (partly considered in the risk assessment). Much of the expenditure identified in items (i) to (iii) has already been incurred or committed and can therefore be regarded as a sunk cost.

*Construction costs*

7.      The estimating techniques used by the UR team for estimating construction costs involve the use of: (i) rates per unit of quantity; (ii) quantities; and (iii) bills of quantities, as described below.   The preparation of estimates for tunnels, route options and on-route stations is also considered below.

*Rates per unit of quantity*

8.      A construction cost database has been established by the UR team using either first principles of estimating, historic data from other rail projects, quotations from contractors/suppliers, estimates from specialist departments within BR or published data. Allowance has then been made in each rate, in the form of varying additional percentages, for preliminaries such as the cost of site establishment, site overheads, work sites and non-attributable temporary works and plant costs.   In many cases, these rates have been consolidated to cover various associated elements of work to form composite rates per unit of quantity, thus avoiding constant repetition of pricing of the constituent quantities of the major elements of the work.   Allowances have been made for construction alongside operating railways.

*Quantities*

9.     Quantities have been measured by the UR team where possible from the engineering drawings available during the development and appraisal stage and have, therefore, had to be refined where drawings have been revised during development of the design.  The engineering plans indicate the optional track routes, the positions of tunnels, tunnel approaches and viaducts.  This has enabled rates to be applied to linear quantities of route in varying conditions e.g. in the open, tunnel, tunnel approaches and viaducts etc. These rates include, where relevant, trackwork, ballast, drainage, utilities, fencing, landscaping, and noise mitigation.  Earthworks quantities have generally been obtained from computer outputs derived from the detailed vertical and horizontal alignment drawings, with adjustments where necessary for removal of unsuitable material below trackwork formations. Over and under-bridges have been priced on a cost per square metre of deck area and footbridges have been enumerated.  Road diversions, diversions and/or crossings of major utilities, and other special cost items have generally been enumerated.  Electrical work, signalling and telecommunications and mechanical work in tunnels have been costed using average rates per kilometre applied to the linear measurement of route in the relevant conditions.

*Bills of Quantities*

10.    Bills of quantities have been produced by the UR team for each section on each of the rural routes appraised, listing the gross quantities and priced using rates from the database.  The resulting totals have then been adjusted to produce estimates expressed in 4Q92 prices (as discussed below).  The estimates for the London section have been compiled in a similar manner.

*Estimates for tunnels*

11.    Estimates for the London and rural tunnels have been compiled from information provided by a national contractor undertaking studies for the Southerly Approach.  The UR team's estimates include for the provision of twin bore tunnels for all tunnels in the London section because of the nature of the ground conditions anticipated on the Easterly Approach. The UR team has assessed that, taking into account the likely cost of structural works necessary to prevent settlement in this built-up section of the route, the twin tunnelling option which has been included in the estimates will be a cheaper alternative than single bore because the smaller diameter twin bore tunnels will create less risk of settlement overall.  An allowance has been made in the estimates for ground improvement and the risk studies have taken account of settlement claims.  The tunnel beneath the Thames is also proposed to be constructed as twin bore to allow acceptable gradients, given UR's current knowledge of the river bed.  The provision of twin bore in lieu of single bore under the Thames has added almost 2% to the cost estimates of each of the main cases.  As no new ground investigations could be undertaken at this stage, the UR team has assumed the use of earth pressure balancing machines for the longer tunnels, the intention being to provide for the worst ground conditions that could be anticipated following studies for earlier tunnel routes. The UR team has assessed likely rates of advance and considered numbers of machines required to complete each tunnel to programme.  Allowances have also been made for ground improvement along the length of tunnels, and for ground improvement around vent and access shafts and cross passages.  The UR team has assumed disposal to tip up to 25 km distant, the most expensive form of disposal of spoil arising from the tunnelling operations.

12.    The ultimate contract strategy, programming constraints and ground investigations will all affect the accuracy of the tunnelling element of the estimate.  In particular, skilful planning and execution of ground investigation is vital to the ultimate success of tunnelling projects.  The UR team recognises this and intends to carry out a review of the approach to tunnel engineering by the appointment of a panel of experts.

*Estimates for route options*

13.    For the London section of the route, to the east of Kings Cross Station and the Barking/Havering border, estimates have been prepared for each engineering drawing produced.  A cost matrix has then been prepared for each distinct length of route, with variants on these for different vertical alignments.  For the remaining rural sections of the route, separate quantities have been produced for each section on each of the routes appraised.

*Estimates for on-route stations*

14.    Options for on-route stations and associated work have been costed separately and presented as additions to the through-route cost.  Designs for the stations have been developed in outline; the sufficiency of the estimates is, therefore, determined by the level of engineering data generated by the UR team.  This approach is appropriate, in our view, taking account of the current stage of the work.

*Project management costs*

15.    In earlier estimates, and those used for the sifting process, a project management allowance was expressed by UR as a percentage addition to the estimated construction costs  The project management allowance in the current UR report comprises a fixed element, common to each of the five case studies, to cover the cost of employment of HQ project staff, the cost of the parliamentary process, the cost of consultations with interested parties and the cost of the BR property board personnel.  This has been calculated using the project milestones given in the report and assumes completion by the year 2000.  A variable, amounting to a 9% addition to the construction cost estimates has then been added to the fixed sum to cover for design, geotechnical investigation and site supervision for each separate case.  This is a reasonable approach to project management costs, in our view.

*Property costs*

16.    The UR team's approach to property costs is as follows:

(i)    Valuations have been prepared for all properties identified on plans prepared by UR engineers as required for the new railway, including cutting and embankment slopes, and sites allocated for construction compounds, temporary offices, etc.

(ii)    The valuations have been prepared following an external inspection of the properties identified as affected, and are based on the acquisition of an unencumbered freehold interest at current prices/values.  They also have regard to statutory compensation rules (as developed by case law).

(iii)   Generally, existing use values have been calculated, but in appropriate cases and where a higher figure would result, valuations have regard to alternative uses either authorised by planning consent or identified in the relevant Local Plans. Agricultural land has been valued on a rate per acre basis. Where the route is tunnelled, it has been assumed that all properties along the line of the cut and cover approaches to each portal will need to be acquired. Otherwise, estimates for the tunnelled sections provide for the acquisition of a perpetual easement only.

(iv)   Allowances have been made for the payment of disturbance claims where appropriate. In those cases where it has been identified as likely that authority will be required to purchase more land than is needed for the scheme (under the material detriment provisions) an allowance for the subsequent resale of the unaffected elements has been made.

(v)   Accommodation works are not allowed for in the property costs. These have been estimated as part of the construction works.

(vi)   Certain properties owned by BR, which are let out to third parties, are costed on the basis that the tenant would receive compensation for dispossession, and also that the railway business would suffer a loss of income.

17.   We have reviewed the methods used to prepare the property costs detailed in the UR report, and found them to be professionally conducted, considering the preliminary nature of the information available to the UR team. The initial review showed that specific risks to the estimates exist as follows:

(i)   Identification of land take. The estimates are based on only that property identified as needed for the currently defined permanent works and construction sites for the reference case. Allowances for temporary construction easements and landscaping will need to be included. However, the UR team has indicated that it expects that the additional cost of such property would be minimal.

(ii)   No allowance has been made for acquisition of residential property outside the immediate line of the works.

(iii)   No specific allowance has been made in the capital cost estimates for compensation claims under Part 1 of the Land Compensation Act where no land is taken.

(iv)   The disturbance allowance of 40% for agricultural and commercial businesses is an estimate.

(v)   The overall state of the property market at the time of the transactions is of crucial importance; also, delays in the disposal of property may affect the property cost estimates.

Property costs amount to less than 5% of the UR estimates, so any effect on the reliability of the overall estimates as a result of risks (i) and (iii) to (v) would be relatively small. Insufficient data have been compiled for us to state categorically that these risks will not make a material difference to the choice between routes. Risk (ii), which concerns blight, could have a material effect on the property cost estimates if a more generous acquisition policy was applied.

*Professionalism of estimate production*

18. The procedures and techniques adopted by the UR team to derive estimates of the capital costs are sound, in our view, and the work to date appears to have generally been carried out in accordance with them. It appears to us, from an examination of selected elements of the estimates, that the work has been executed in a professional manner and is at a level commensurate with the current stage of development of the design.

## Project timescale and construction programme

19. The UR team has assumed an outline construction programme which allows completion of CTRL early in the year 2000. This programme takes account of tunnel driving needs, spoil disposal methods and construction work packaging.

20. It is accepted by the UR team that specific measures need to be taken during the period from now until Royal Assent to the Bill (or approval under an alternative procedure) in order to achieve completion by the year 2000. It is not clear how approval of the project under an alternative procedure would affect the planned completion by the year 2000. These measures include the early preparation of a construction method statement and mass-haul curves for the earthmoving operations, to assist in detailed planning of the construction work packages. Additionally it is proposed that a comprehensive review of tunnelling requirements and techniques is carried out by specialist engineering consultants, tunnelling contractors and tunnel boring machine ('TBM') manufacturers, in order to establish specifications for the TBMs.

21. There is a critical assumption in the construction programme, that it will be possible to commit a certain level of funds and procure various work and supplies before Royal Assent is obtained. This would include procurement and manufacture of TBMs and the relocation of the high voltage DC Cable at Sellinge. Also significant advance works and enabling works will need to be committed. All geotechnical surveys will need to be complete and the civil works will have to be fully designed and tenders sought and appraised ready for contract commencement immediately on receipt of Royal Assent. The UR team has estimated that the amount of these commitments prior to Royal Assent might approach 13% of the capital cost estimates for each case. Primary factors in the success of these proposals are the establishment of appropriate procurement plans and contractor pre-selection procedures, together with comprehensive project management and supervision procedures backed by suitable project control techniques.

22. There are inherent risks in the proposed approach. All work committed before the completion of the consultation process or Royal Assent is at risk to some extent. Delays during the pre-construction phase will put funds at risk up to the total cost of the design and management team and its support costs. Delays after construction commences will additionally put funds at risk to the extent of the construction contractors' costs and UR supervisors' costs. A further risk identified is the short period of time allowed for commissioning and testing. These risks could affect the reliability of the overall estimates but should not affect the choice between routes.

WSA

## ANNEX E: RELIABILITY OF THE CAPITAL COST ESTIMATES AND RISK ANALYSIS

1.    The base estimates produced for the various cases make no allowance for contingencies, design cost growth, unforeseen circumstances or other internal or external risks.  The UR team's remit requires them to commission a risk assessment to look at the robustness of the cost and revenue forecasts, including an assessment of the timetable.  The risk assessment is designed to predict a range of prices against a probability of achievement, and replaces the coarse addition of percentage allowances for contingencies.  The basic techniques applied are iterative.  The Risk Specialists prepare a risk log after discussion and review with key team members.  An early issue of the risk register has been made available for our review.  The data are modelled using standard software in order to predict ranges of cost estimates for given assumptions.

2.    The approach to the risk appraisal uses standard techniques.  Judgements need to be made about the way in which such techniques should be applied to the design and construction process and the conventions for contractual risk sharing in the civil engineering sector.  We are not convinced that residual risk items, such as the impact of poor ground on the cost of tunnelling and earthworks, have been given the priority they deserve when considered against the contract risk assumptions used in building up the base cost estimate.  The modelling techniques adopted may have taken these items into account but these have not been made available to us for review.

3.    The risk assessment has segmented the project geographically.  The assessment identifies the area which is most vulnerable to cost inaccuracy and requires the greatest focus during the next stage of development as being Section 1 in all cases except the additional tunnels options of the route 301 alignment where Section 3 becomes the most vulnerable.  The ongoing process of allocating ownership of risks identified has thus commenced and should be continued as a proactive management tool.  A further study, segmenting the project by engineering element rather than location, is recommended.  This would provide focus on the facets of the whole project which require attention.

4.    A margin of error in the range of -10% to +30% is normal for a project of this type at this stage of development.  This is the percentage spread which UR had considered before the introduction of the risk appraisal process.  The formal risk assessment undertaken by the UR team indicates a range of -10% to +22% around the basic estimated cost of the Board Reference Case, within 95% confidence limits.  However, UR's work so far does not include a risk appraisal of the construction programme; we understand that the UR team intends to carry out shortly an assessment of the risk of delay in the construction programme.  We have conducted a high level review of the main risk areas of the project, both geographically and by engineering element.  This is akin to rationalising a simple percentage addition for contingency.  On the basis of this review, we do not consider that the margin of error of the estimated capital cost should be assumed to be less than the range of -10% to +30% which is normal for a project of this type at this stage of development.  This margin will need to be reviewed when details of the London terminal, the risk registers and the detailed construction programme are available.

WSA